George Melville Baker

Ballads of Beauty

George Melville Baker

Ballads of Beauty

ISBN/EAN: 9783743306783

Manufactured in Europe, USA, Canada, Australia, Japa

Cover: Foto ©ninafisch / pixelio.de

Manufactured and distributed by brebook publishing software (www.brebook.com)

George Melville Baker

Ballads of Beauty

Contents.

	PAGE
BEAUTY. — *Young*	13
WAITING IN THE TWILIGHT. — *Alice M. Adams*	14
LIFE SONGS. — *Amy Key*	18
THE WELCOME. — *Thomas Davis*	25
LOVE AT FIRST SIGHT. — *Edward Bulwer Lytton*	26
O FAIREST OF THE RURAL MAIDS. — *William Cullen Bryant*	30
LOUISE ON THE DOORSTEP. — *Charles Mackay*	37
OUR SKATER BELLE. — *Anonymous*	38
AUGUSTA. — *Saxe*	42
LORD ULLIN'S DAUGHTER. — *Thomas Campbell*	45
WINTER SONG	50
THE MILLER'S DAUGHTER. — *Alfred Tennyson*	54

CONTENTS.

	PAGE
OH, WERE MY LOVE A COUNTRY LASS. — *William Allingham*	58
THE SIESTA. — *William Cullen Bryant*	62
THE QUEEN'S RIDE. — *Thomas Bailey Aldrich*	66
MARY MORISON. — *Robert Burns*	70
MARGARET AND DORA. — *Thomas Campbell*	74
OUT IN THE COLD. — "*Fair Women*"	77
THE ANNOYER. — *N. P. Willis*	82
DESOLATE. — *Gerald Massey*	86
LINGER, O GENTLE TIME	90
BONNIE BESSIE. — *George S. Burleigh*	94
THE CONFIDANTE. — "*Fair Women*"	98
SOMEBODY'S WAITING FOR SOMEBODY. — *Charles Swain*	102
ELISE. — *Henry Gillman*	106
SOMEBODY. — *Anonymous*	110
A TRUE WOMAN. — *William Wordsworth*	114
FLOWERS AND FLOWERS. — "*Fair Women*"	118
SHE WALKS IN BEAUTY. — *Lord Byron*	122
MY SUNSHINE. — *S. P. Driver*	126
A SLEEPING BEAUTY. — *Samuel Rogers*	130

CONTENTS.

	PAGE
THE LADY'S "YES." — *Elizabeth Barrett Browning*	134
A HEALTH. — *Edward Coate Pinkney*	138
WINIFRED'S HAIR. — *Hamilton Aïdé*	142
IN THE ORGAN LOFT. — *George Arnold*	146
A GARDEN IN HER FACE. — *Richard Allison*	150
WHEN STARS ARE IN THE QUIET SKIES. — *Edward Bulwer Lytton*	154
THE TIME I'VE LOST IN WOOING. — *Thomas Moore*	158
NOT A MATCH. — *Henry S. Leigh*	162
OH, SAW YE THE LASS. — *Richard Ryan*	166

Ballads of Beauty.

BEAUTY.

BEAUTY gives
The features perfectness, and to the form
Its delicate proportions: she may stain
The eye with a celestial blue, the cheek
With carmine of the sunset; she may breathe
Grace into every motion, like the play
Of the least visible tissue of a cloud;
She may give all that's rich — her own
Bright cestus — and one glance of Intellect,
Like stronger magic, will outshine it all.

Waiting in the Twilight.

SLOWLY from the western hill-sides
   Fades the sunset's ruddy light,
While the birds amid the tree-tops
   Softly chirp their sweet "Good-night."

Where the elm trees' spreading branches
   Hide the streamlets with their shades,
Stands the fair-faced, blue-eyed Dolly,
   Flower of all the village maids, —

Looking, in the growing twilight,
   Towards the grassy fields ahead,
Listening still, with eye expectant,
   For the ever-welcome tread.

From across the verdant meadow
   Comes a whistle, loud and shrill,
Sounding through the evening stillness,
   Seemeth but the whip-poor-will.

But the fair face glows still brighter,
   And the eyes more eager grow,
As the notes come near and nearer,
   Louder than the streamlet's flow.

WAITING IN THE TWILIGHT.

Soon she hears the well-known music
  Of his voice, borne on the air:
"Don't you hear me coming, Dolly?
  Dolly, dear, I'll soon be there."

And the one she's long been waiting,
  Hat upraised, now comes in sight,
Hastening towards the blue-eyed maiden,
  Waiting in the soft twilight.

Happy hearts, so young and trusting,
  May no frost e'er blight your love,
But may blessings all unnumbered
  Fall upon you from above!

Life Songs.

A BROOK flashed from a rugged height,
    Merrily, merrily glancing;
The songs of the summer light
    Kept time to the tune of its dancing.
Fond eyes looked on its dewy sheen,
    Reading fate in its waters;
"Darling, the song of the brook is for you,
    Fairest of earth's dear daughters."
Bright eyes looked on its dewy sheen,
    And the songs of their lives rang clearly,—
"The world is fair! the world is fair!"
    "And I love, I love you dearly."

Autumn leaves, like a fairy fleet,
    Swept down towards the river;
The false wind moaned through the dreary sleet,
    "The flowers are dead forever!"
Sad eyes looked down on the shadowed stream,
    Reading fate in its measure;
"For me your song, for my withered life,
    Pain in the mask of pleasure."
Sad eyes looked on the shadowed stream,
    And the songs of their lives rang clearly,—
"The world is sad! the world is sad!"
    "Oh! I loved, I loved him dearly."

LIFE SONGS.

A flush, a glow on the winter skies,
    Earth smiles in her happy dreaming;
Whispers the wind, "Arise! arise!
    The dawn of spring is beaming."
Calm eyes look down on the sunny brook,
    With a smile that has conquered sadness —
"Your song is for me in this sweet spring-time,
    In heaven is perfect gladness."
Calm eyes look on its dewy sheen,
    And the songs of their lives ring gayly, —
"The spring is here! the spring is here!"
    "I find strength for my burden daily."

The Welcome.

I.

COME in the evening or come in the morning,
    Come when you're looked for or come without warning,
    Kisses and welcome you'll find here before you,
And the oftener you come here the more I'll adore you!
  Light is my heart since the day we were plighted,
  Red is my cheek that they told me was blighted;
  The green of the trees looks far greener than ever,
  And the linnets are singing, "True lovers don't sever!"

II.

I'll pull you sweet flowers, to wear if you choose them,
Or, after you've kissed them, they'll lie on my bosom;
I'll fetch from the mountain its breeze to inspire you;
I'll fetch from my fancy a tale that won't tire you.
  Oh! your step's like the rain to the summer-vexed farmer,
  Or sabre and shield to a knight without armor.
  I'll sing you sweet songs till the stars rise above me,
  Then, wandering, I'll wish you in silence to love me.

III.

We'll look through the trees at the cliff and the eyrie;
We'll tread round the rath on the track of the fairy;

THE WELCOME.

We'll look on the stars, and we'll list to the river,
Till you ask of your darling what gift you can give her.
   Oh! she'll whisper you, — "Love, as unchangeably beaming,
   And trust, when in secret, most tunefully streaming,
   Till the starlight of heaven above us shall quiver,
   As our souls flow in one down eternity's river."

IV.

So come in the evening or come in the morning,
Come when you're looked for or come without warning.
Kisses and welcome you'll find here before you,
And the oftener you come here the more I'll adore you!
   Light is my heart since the day we were plighted,
   Red is my cheek that they told me was blighted;
   The green of the trees looks far greener than ever,
   And the linnets are singing, "True lovers don't sever!"

LOVE AT FIRST SIGHT.

NTO my heart a silent look
　　Flashed from thy careless eyes;
And what before was shadow, took
　　The light of summer skies.
The first-born Love was in that look;
The Venus rose from out the deep
　　Of those inspiring eyes.

My life, like some lone, solemn spot
　　A spirit passes o'er,
Grew instinct with a glory not
　　In earth or heaven before.
Sweet trouble stirred the haunted spot,
And shook the leaves of every thought
　　Thy presence wandered o'er!

My being yearned, and crept to thine,
　　As if in times of yore
Thy soul had been a part of mine,
　　Which claimed it back once more —
Thy very self no longer thine,
But merged in that delicious life
　　Which made us ONE of yore!

LOVE AT FIRST SIGHT.

There bloomed beside thee forms as fair,
   There murmured tones as sweet :
But round thee breathed the enchanted air
   'T was life and death to meet.
And henceforth thou alone wert fair,
And though the stars had sung for joy,
   Thy whisper only sweet !

O Fairest of the Rural Maids.

FAIREST of the rural maids!
Thy birth was in the forest shades;
Green boughs, and glimpses of the sky,
Were all that met thine infant eye.

Thy sports, thy wanderings, when a child,
Were ever in the sylvan wild;
And all the beauty of the place
Is in thy heart and on thy face.

The twilight of the trees and rocks
Is in the light shade of thy locks;
Thy step is as the wind, that weaves
Its playful way among the leaves.

Thine eyes are springs, in whose serene
And silent waters heaven is seen;
Their lashes are the herbs that look
On their young figures in the brook.

The forest depths, by foot unpressed,
Are not more sinless than thy breast:
The holy peace that fills the air
Of those calm solitudes, is there.

Louise on the Doorstep.

HALF-PAST three in the morning!
    And no one in the street
But me, on the sheltering doorstep
    Resting my weary feet,
Watching the rain-drops patter
    And dance where the puddles run,
As bright in the flaring gas-light
    As dew-drops in the sun.

There's a light upon the pavement,
    It shines like a magic glass,
And there are faces in it
    That look at me and pass.
Faces — ah! well remembered
    In the happy Long Ago,
When my garb was white as lilies,
    And my thoughts as pure as snow.

Faces! ah, yes! I see them —
    One, two, and three — and four —
That come in the gust of tempests,
    And go on the winds that bore.
Changeful and evanescent,
    They shine mid storm and rain,

Till the terror of their beauty
    Lies deep upon my brain.

One of them frowns; *I* know him,
    With his thin, long, snow-white hair, —
Cursing his wretched daughter
    That drove him to despair.
And the other, with wakening pity
    In her large, tear-streaming eyes,
Seems as she yearned towards me,
    And whispered " Paradise."

They pass, — they melt in the ripples,
    And I shut mine eyes, that burn,
To escape another vision
    That follows where 'er I turn —
The face of a false deceiver
    That lives and lies; ah, me!
Though I see it in the pavement,
    Mocking my misery!

They are gone, all three! — quite vanished!
    Let nothing call them back!
For I've had enough of phantoms,
    And my heart is on the rack.
God help me in my sorrow!
    But *there*, — in the wet, cold stone,
Smiling in heavenly beauty,
    I see my lost, mine own!

There, on the glimmering pavement,
    With eyes as blue as morn,

Floats by the fair-haired darling
    Too soon from my bosom torn.
She clasps her tiny fingers,
    She calls me sweet and mild,
And says that my God forgives me
    For the sake of my little child.

I will go to her grave to-morrow,
    And pray that I may die ;
And I hope that my God will take me
    Ere the days of my youth go by.
For I am old in anguish,
    And long to be at rest,
With my little babe beside me,
    And the daisies on my breast.

OUR SKATER BELLE.

ALONG the frozen lake she comes
   In linking crescents, light and fleet;
The ice-imprisoned Undine hums
   A welcome to her little feet.

I see the jaunty hat, the plume
   Swerve bird-like in the joyous gale,—
The cheeks lit up to burning bloom,
   The young eyes sparkling through the veil.

The quick breath parts her laughing lips,
   The white neck shines through tossing curls;
Her vesture gently sways and dips,
   As on she speeds in shell-like whorls.

Men stop and smile to see her go;
   They gaze, they smile in pleased surprise;
They ask her name; they long to show
   Some silent friendship in their eyes.

She glances not; she passes on;
   Her steely footfall quicker rings;
She guesses not the benison
   Which follows her on noiseless wings.

OUR SKATER BELLE.

Smooth be her ways, secure her tread,
  Along the devious lines of life,
From grace to grace successive led, —
  A noble maiden, nobler wife!

Augusta.

"HANDSOME and haughty!" a comment that came
   From lips which were never accustomed to malice:
A girl with a presence superb as her name,
   And charmingly fitted for love — in a palace!
And oft I have wished — for in musing alone
   One's fancy is apt to be very erratic —
That the lady might wear — No! I never will own
   A thought so decidedly undemocratic!
But *if* 't were a *coronet* — this, I 'll aver,
   No duchess on earth could more gracefully wear it;
And even a democrat — thinking of *her* —
   Might surely be pardoned for wishing to share it!

Lord Ullin's Daughter.

A CHIEFTAIN to the Highlands bound,
    Cries, "Boatman, do not tarry!
And I 'll give thee a silver pound
    To row us o'er the ferry."

"Now who be ye would cross Lochgyle,
    This dark and stormy water?"
"Oh, I 'm the chief of Ulva's isle,
    And this Lord Ullin's daughter.

"And fast before her father's men
    Three days we 've fled together;
For should he find us in the glen,
    My blood would stain the heather.

"His horsemen hard behind us ride;
    Should they our steps discover,
Then who will cheer my bonny bride
    When they have slain her lover?"

Out spoke the hardy Highland wight,
    "I 'll go, my chief, — I 'm ready;
It is not for your silver bright,
    But for your winsome lady.

"And by my word! the bonny bird
 In danger shall not tarry;
So though the waves are raging white,
 I'll row you o'er the ferry."

By this the storm grew loud apace,
 The water-wraith was shrieking;
And in the scowl of heaven each face
 Grew dark as they were speaking.

But still, as wilder blew the wind,
 And as the night grew drearer,
Adown the glen rode arméd men,
 Their trampling sounded nearer.

"Oh, haste thee, haste!" the lady cries,
 "Though tempests round us gather;
I'll meet the raging of the skies,
 But not an angry father."

The boat has left a stormy land,
 A stormy sea before her,
When, oh! too strong for human hand
 The tempest gathered o'er her.

And still they rowed amidst the roar
 Of waters fast prevailing;
Lord Ullin reached that fatal shore:
 His wrath was changed to wailing.

For sore dismayed, through storm and shade,
 His child he did discover;
One lovely hand she stretched for aid,
 And one was round her lover.

"Come back! come back!" he cried, in grief,
  "Across this stormy water,
And I'll forgive your Highland chief,
  My daughter! O my daughter!"

'T was vain; the loud waves lashed the shore,
  Return or aid preventing;
The waters wild went o'er his child,
  And he was left lamenting.

Winter Song.

INTRY winds are calling,
    Whereso'er I go;
Dismally is falling,
    The melancholy snow!
Birds from off the bough,
    Long have taken flight;
There is no singing now,
    And scant sunlight.
I weary for the old days,
    When all the world looked gay;
These are the cold days,—
    Summer hath fled away!

Love and peace and gladness,
    Stayed a little space;
Solitude and sadness
    Meet me in their place.
Love passed idly by,
    Soon was gladness flown;
Peace was last to fly,—
    I am alone!
And I weary for the old days,
    And those who would not stay;
These are the cold days,—
    Summer hath fled away!

WINTER SONG.

Heart! hast thou a reason
    Thus to throb and yearn
In the wintry season?
    Why should he return
In the wintry hours?
    'T is too late to gain
One who mid the flowers
    Would not remain.
And I weary for the old days,
    And one who would not stay;
These are the cold days, —
    Summer hath fled away!

The Miller's Daughter.

'T is the miller's daughter,
    And she is grown so dear, so dear,
That I would be the jewel
    That trembles at her ear;
For, hid in ringlets day and night,
I 'd touch her neck so warm and white.

And I would be the girdle
    About her dainty, dainty waist,
And her heart would beat against me
    In sorrow and in rest;
And I should know if it beat right,
I 'd clasp it round so close and tight.

And I would be the necklace,
    And all day long to fall and rise

Upon her balmy bosom
  With her laughter or her sighs;
And I would lie so light, so light,
I scarce should be unclasped at night.

Oh, were my Love a Country Lass.

Oh, were my love a country lass,
    That I might see her every day;
And sit with her on hedge-row grass
    Beneath a bough of May;
And find her cattle when astray,
    Or help to drive them to the field,
And linger on our homeward way,
    And woo her lips to yield
A twilight kiss before we parted,
Full of love, yet easy-hearted!

Oh, were my love a cottage maid,
    To spin through many a winter night,
Where ingle-corner lends its shade
    From fir-wood blazing bright.
Beside her wheel what dear delight
    To watch the blushes go and come,
With tender words that took no fright
    Beneath the friendly hum;
Or rising smile, or tear-drop swelling,
At a fireside legend's telling!

OH, WERE MY LOVE A COUNTRY LASS.

Oh, were my love a peasant girl,
　That never saw the wicked town;
Was never dight with silk or pearl,
　But graced a homely gown.
How less than weak were fashion's frown
　To vex our unambitious lot!
How rich were love and peace to crown
　Our green secluded cot,
Where age would come serene and shining,
Like an autumn day's declining!

THE SIESTA.

(FROM THE SPANISH.)

IRS! that wander and murmur round,
    Bearing delight where'er ye blow,
Make in the elms a lulling sound,
    While my lady sleeps in the shade below.

Lighten and lengthen her noonday rest,
    Till the heat of the noonday sun is o'er;
Sweet be her slumbers, — though in my breast
    The pain she has waked may slumber no more.
Breathing soft from the blue profound,
    Bearing delight where'er ye blow,
Make in the elms a lulling sound,
    While my lady sleeps in the shade below.

Airs! that over the bending boughs,
    And under the shade of pendent leaves,

THE SIESTA.

Murmur soft, like my timid vows,
  Or the secret sighs my bosom heaves, —
Gently sweeping the grassy ground,
  Bearing delight where'er ye blow,
Make in the elms a lulling sound,
  While my lady sleeps in the shade below.

THE QUEEN'S RIDE.

'TIS that fair time of year,
      Lady mine!
When stately Guinevere
  In her sea-green robe and hood,
Went a-riding through the wood,
      Lady mine!

And as the Queen did ride,
      Lady mine!
Sir Launcelot at her side
Laughed and chatted, bending over,
Half her friend and all her lover,
      Lady mine!

And as they rode along,
      Lady mine!
The throstle gave them song,
And the buds peeped through the grass
To see youth and beauty pass,
      Lady mine!

And on, through deathless time,
    Lady mine !
These lovers in their prime
(Two fairy ghosts together !)
Ride, with sea-green robe and feather,
    Lady mine !

And so we two will ride,
    Lady mine !
At your pleasure, side by side,
Laugh and chat, — I bending over,
Half your friend and all your lover,
    Lady mine !

But if you like not this,
    Lady mine !
And take my love amiss,
Then I 'll ride unto the end,
Half your lover, all your friend,
    Lady mine !

So come which way you will,
    Lady mine !
Vale, upland, plain, and hill
Wait your coming. For one day
Loose the bridle, and away !
    Lady mine !

MARY MORISON.

MARY, at thy window be —
    It is the wished, the trysted hour!
Those smiles and glances let me see
    That make the miser's treasure poor.
How blithely wad I bide the stoure,
    A weary slave frae sun to sun,
Could I the rich reward secure,
    Of lovely Mary Morison!

Yestreen, when to the trembling string
    The dance gaed through the lighted ha',
To thee my fancy took its wing, —
    I sat, but neither heard nor saw,
Though this was fair, and that was braw,
    And you the toast of a' the town,
I sighed, and said, amang them a',
    Ye are na Mary Morison!

O Mary, canst thou wreck his peace
    Wha for thy sake wad gladly die?

Or canst thou break that heart of his,
  Whase only faut is loving thee?
If love for love thou wilt na gie,
  At least be pity to me shown:
A thought ungentle canna be
  The thought of Mary Morison.

Margaret' and Dora.

ARGARET'S beauteous, — Grecian arts
   Ne'er drew form completer;
Yet why, in my heart of hearts,
   Hold I Dora's sweeter?

Dora's eyes of heavenly blue
   Pass all painting's reach, —
Ringdoves' notes are discord to
   The music of her speech.

Artists! Margaret's smile receive,
   And on canvas show it;
But for perfect worship, leave
   Dora to her poet.

Out in the Cold.

UNDER a bough without berries or leaves,
Where the keen winter's slave silver webs weaves,
Where the bleak, bitter blast swoops o'er the hill,
Where the swift-flying flake never is still,
      Maidens three,
      Here are we,
         Surely not old.
      Pity us,
      Succor us,
         Out in the cold!

New Year's morn tempted us out in the snow,
Rudely the blast came down, making cheeks glow,
Snatching at wrap and veil, seeking to hurl
Dead leaf and flake at us, tangled each curl.
      Company
      Maidens three
         Are not, 't is told;
      'T is not fair;
      We despair,
         Out in the cold.

BALLADS OF BEAUTY.

Shelter we seek in vain here mid the storm,
Waiting most patiently some welcome warm ;
'T is but a secret to you told apart —
The shelter that we would have lies in some heart.
        Sad our lot,
        Blame us not,
            Think us not bold ;
        Even Eve
        Sure would grieve,
            Left in the cold.

Who has not told of the tendril-tipped vine,
Breathed of the blossoms in poetry's line,
Vowed that the former needs where it may twine,
And the latter a stay where its petals may shine?
        Yet alone
        Here we moan
            Troubles untold ;
        Blossoms pale,
        Vine a-trail,
            Out in the cold.

But hark ! there are steps coming over the snow,
To set our hearts beating and make our cheeks glow ;

And yet how a-tremble each one falls again,
As longing hearts ponder on flight by the lane!
      Yet elate,
       'T is too late;
         Eager and bold
      Three appear —
     Nay, are here,
        Out in the cold.

THE ANNOYER.

OVE knoweth every form of air,
    And every shape of earth,
And comes, unbidden, everywhere,
    Like thought's mysterious birth.
The moonlit sea and the sunset sky
    Are written with Love's words,
And you hear his voice unceasingly,
    Like song, in the time of birds.

He peeps into the warrior's heart,
    From the tip of a stooping plume,
And the serried spears, and the many men,
    May not deny him room.
He'll come to his tent in the weary night,
    And be busy in his dream,
And he'll float to his eye in morning light,
    Like a fay on a silver beam.

He hears the sound of the hunter's gun,
    And rides on the echo back,
And sighs in his ear like a stirring leaf
    And flits in his woodland track.

The shade of the wood and the sheen of the river,
    The cloud and the open sky,—
He will haunt them all with his subtle quiver,
    Like the light of your very eye.

He blurs the print of the scholar's book,
    And intrudes in the maiden's prayer,
And profanes the cell of the holy man
    In the shape of a lady fair.
In the darkest night and the bright daylight,
    In earth, and sea, and sky,
In every home of human thought,
    Will Love be lurking nigh.

Desolate.

THE day goes down red, darkling,
   The moaning waves dash out the light,
And there is not a star of hope sparkling
   On the threshold of my night.

Wild winds of Autumn go wailing
   Up the valley and over the hill,
Like yearning ghosts round the world sailing,
   In search of the old love still.

A fathomless sea is rolling
   O'er the wreck of the bravest bark;
And my pain-muffled heart is tolling
   Its dumb peal down in the dark.

The waves of a mighty sorrow
   Have whelmèd the pearl of my life;
And there cometh to me no morrow
   Shall solace this desolate strife.

DESOLATE.

Gone are the last faint flashes,
   Set is the sun of my years;
And over a few poor ashes
   I sit in my darkness and tears.

Linger, O Gentle Time.

LINGER, O gentle Time,
Linger, O radiant grace of bright to-day!
   Let not the hours' chime
     Call thee away,
But linger near me still with fond delay.

   Linger, for thou art mine!
What dearer treasures can the Future hold?
   What sweeter flowers than thine
     Can she unfold?
What secret tell my heart thou hast not told?

   Oh, linger in thy flight!
For shadows gather round, and should we part,
   A dreary, stirless night
     May fill my heart.
Then pause and linger yet ere thou depart.

LINGER, O GENTLE TIME.

Linger, I ask no more.
Thou art enough forever — thou alone.
What Future can restore
When thou art flown,
All that I hold for thee and call my own?

BONNIE BESSIE.

I LOVE Bessie and she loves me —
Bonnie Bessie, who lives by the sea,
Sweet and lovely as lass can be ;
White and rosy, with eyes of blue,
Luminous eyes, like globes of dew, —
You see the morning firmament through !
Light and grace in her motion free,
Sweetest lady of all I see,
For I love Bessie and she loves me !

Some have houses, and some have stocks,
And some have treasure in veinéd rocks,
And some heap gold in an iron box ;
Cattle and horses and sheep have some ;
For another his great ships go and come,
And a hundred mills for his brother hum ;
But I, who have only an eye to see
And a heart to bless her, can happier be,
For I love Bessie and she loves me !

BONNIE BESSIE.

One flaunts a title before his name,
And one behind his, — both for the same, —
Baggage checked to the Station of Fame!
Office and honors, ribbons and fees,
Some for those, and others for these,
Wrestle and run in the mire to their knees;
But I, with only a name that she
Makes musical, can happier be,
For I love Bessie and she loves me!

My lady is eight years old to-day,
A stave of music that danced away
In a fairy's form, — a morning ray
Involved in vapors of misty pearl,
That flushed and throbbed in a dainty whirl,
Till it stepped to earth a living girl,
With the sun-steeped mist yet rippling free,
For her golden hair! my bliss to be,
For I love Bessie and she loves me!

I see by the glass that Time has tossed
Over my locks his powdery frost;
But whoot, old man, your labor is lost!
For every day you lessen the way
Between me and my delicate fay,
My bonny, bounding Bessie Grey;
Years may whiten what white may be,
But the heart she lightens is young as she,
For I love Bessie and she loves me!

THE CONFIDANTE.

I.

LETTER, Lucy? for me to read?
    Ah, tell-tale blushes, what secret now?
I am but teasing.   There, never heed,
    Nor blur with furrows that little brow.

II.

Yes, as I thought.   'T is the old, old tale :
    He loves you ; dreams of you night and day ;
With hope he brightens, with dread turns pale, —
    Truths, dear sister, or babblings gray.

III.

Love lives forever, if heart-born, real ;
    But fades like the roses I 've now just clipped,
When told by one who your peace would steal,
    Then flit to some blossom as honey-lipped.

IV.

To you each word here is truth's own mint :
    To me, once cheated, there 's room for doubt ;
You, sister, could him give your love *sans* stint —
    What, tears and trembling ? a dawning pout ?

V.

Yes, as I thought. 'Tis the old, old tale:
  He loves you; dreams of you night and day;
With hope he brightens, with dread turns pale, —
  Truths, dear sister, or babblings gray.

VI.

Well, darling, believe then, and cynic thought
  Shall fade away in your love's sweet sun.
He is not worldly nor fashion-taught;
  I would not darken new light begun.

VII.

His words are manly; an honest ring
  Sounds in each sentence. Ah! Lucy, live
Long in the love that can never wing,
  Whilst I — well, yes — I have yet to give.

Somebody's Waiting for Somebody.

RAINY and rough sets the day, —
    There's a heart beating for somebody;
I must be up and away, —
    Somebody's anxious for somebody.
Thrice hath she been to the gate,
    Thrice hath she listened for somebody.
Midst the night, stormy and late,
    Somebody's waiting for somebody.

There'll be a comforting fire,
    There'll be a welcome for somebody;
One, in her neatest attire,
    Will look at the table for somebody.
Though the stars fled from the west,
    There is a star yet for somebody,
Lighting the home he loves best,
    Warming the bosom of somebody.

There'll be a coat o'er the chair,
    There will be slippers for somebody;

There 'll be a wife's tender care, —
  Love's fond embracement for somebody:
There 'll be the little one's charms, —
  Soon 't will be wakened for somebody.
When I have both in my arms,
  Oh! but how blest will be somebody.

ELISE.

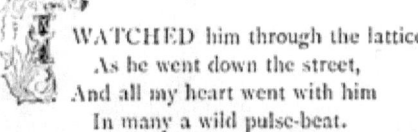

WATCHED him through the lattice
  As he went down the street,
And all my heart went with him
  In many a wild pulse-beat.

'T was in the gentle spring-time,
  At the vanishing of snow,
And my sullen, stagnant nature
  Began to bloom and blow —

Began to feel within it
  Rise a strange, unearthly power,
As the perfume rises softly
  In the newly-opened flower.

He brought me buds and blossoms,
  He brought me gladness, too;
And I told him — told him truly,
  When he came to woo.

ELISE.

A heaven on earth, my master!
   My gracious lord, my king!
I knew thee when I saw thee,
   And thy voice made silence ring.

The silences within me,
   That never had been broke,
Passed into mystic music;
   They heard thee, and awoke.

The world says I am fickle,
   And that my heart is stone,
But I feel through all my being
   That my soul and his are one.

His greatness ever lifts me
   Where holier light is given.
How weak are thanks for blessings
   Which shall endure in heaven!

Somebody.

SOMEBODY'S courting somebody,
　　Somewhere or other to-night;
Somebody's whispering to somebody,
Somebody's listening to somebody,
　　Under this clear moonlight.

Near the bright river's flow,
Running so still and slow,
Talking so soft and low,
　　She sits with somebody.

Pacing the ocean's shore,
Edged by the foaming roar,
Words never used before
　　Sound sweet to somebody.

Under the maple-tree,
Deep though the shadow be,
Plain enough they can see,
　　Bright eyes has somebody.

SOMEBODY.

No one sits up to wait,
Though she is out so late,
All know she's at the gate,
   Talking with somebody.

Tiptoe to parlor door,
Two shadows on the floor,
Moonlight, reveal no more,
   Susy and somebody.

Two, sitting side by side,
Float with the ebbing tide, —
" Thus, dearest, may we glide
   Through life," says somebody.

Somewhere, somebody
Makes love to somebody,
   To-night.

A TRUE WOMAN.

HE was a phantom of delight
When first she gleamed upon my sight;
A lovely apparition, sent
To be a moment's ornament;
Her eyes as stars of twilight fair,
Like twilight's, too, her dusky hair;
But all things else about her drawn
From May-time and the cheerful dawn;
A dancing shape, an image gay,
To haunt, to startle, and waylay.

I saw her upon nearer view,
A spirit, yet a woman too!
Her household motions light and free,
And steps of virgin liberty;
A countenance in which did meet
Sweet records, promises as sweet;
A creature not too bright or good
For human nature's daily food,
For transient sorrows, simple wiles,
Praise, blame, love, kisses, tears, and smiles.

A TRUE WOMAN.

And now I see with eye serene
The very pulse of the machine ;
A being breathing thoughtful breath,
A traveller betwixt life and death ;
The reason firm, the temperate will,
Endurance, foresight, strength, and skill ;
A perfect woman, nobly planned,
To warn, to comfort, and command ;
And yet a spirit still, and bright
With something of an angel light.

Flowers, and Flowers.

Beautiful flowers,
  In feathery bowers,
Filling the air with a silent perfume;
   Sweet garden of roses,
   Your beauty discloses
A charm to subdue the soul's sadness and gloom.

  From rich parterre,
  Or where city air,
Though dank and noisome, hath left you living,
   Ye come together
   In the summer weather,
To praise His name who is ever giving.

  Oh, the joy and grace
  That enrich the place
Where your manifold tints and odors are spread!
   Bewitching and rare,
   Ye make the land fair
As the Garden of Eden long mourned as dead.

FLOWERS, AND FLOWERS.

Beautiful girls!
England's fair pearls,
Whose hands are lilies, whose cheeks are roses,
These upturned faces
Of flower-graces
Are uttering sounds as their life disposes.

They lead you through
Yon sunny blue,
A link 'twixt earth and the angel-powers,
And seem to say,
Singing day by day,
"God make you blossom and bloom like the flowers."

SHE WALKS IN BEAUTY.

SHE walks in beauty, like the night
   Of cloudless climes and starry skies;
And all that's best of dark and bright
   Meets in her aspect and her eyes;
Thus mellowed to that tender light
   Which heaven to gaudy day denies.

One shade the more, one ray the less,
   Had half impaired the nameless grace
Which waves in every raven tress,
   Or softly lightens o'er her face,—
Where thoughts serenely sweet express
   How pure, how dear, their dwelling-place.

And on that cheek, and o'er that brow,
   So soft, so calm, yet eloquent,

SHE WALKS IN BEAUTY.

The smiles that win, the tints that glow,
   But tell of days in goodness spent —
A mind at peace with all below,
   A heart whose love is innocent.

My Sunshine.

IKE a cluster of sunbeams her hair is,
  As blue as the sky-tints her eye,
And I think of the Queen of the Fairies
  Whenever she passes me by;
    And if we had fays
    Flitting round nowadays,
I should *fear* she might fly far away
        Some day.

Sometimes I am puzzled with wonder,
  To know why the wings were left out;
But I'm pleased that they made such a blunder,
  When the little one first came about;
    For if she had wings,
    And soft feathers and things,
I should *know* she would fly far away
        Some day.

MY SUNSHINE.

I suspect, after all, she's but human;
  Yet an angel I could n't love more.
She's a sunshiny, sweet little woman,
  And her heart is a wide-open door.
    Oh, may never a sin,
        Through that door enter in!
    For I know she *will* fly far away
                Some day.

A Sleeping Beauty.

SLEEP on, and dream of Heaven awhile!
   Though shut so close thy laughing eyes,
Thy rosy lips still wear a smile,
   And move and breathe delicious sighs.

Ah! now soft blushes tinge her cheeks
   And mantle o'er her neck of snow;
Ah! now she murmurs, now she speaks,
   What most I wish, and fear to know.

She starts, she trembles, and she weeps,
   Her fair hands folded on her breast;
And now, how like a saint she sleeps,
   A seraph in the realms of rest!

A SLEEPING BEAUTY.

Sleep on secure! Above control,
   Thy thoughts belong to Heaven and thee;
And may the secret of thy soul
   Remain within its sanctuary!

The Lady's Yes.

"YES!" I answered you last night;
   "No!" this morning, sir, I say.
Colors seen by candle-light
   Will not look the same by day.

When the tabors played their best,
   Lamps above and laughs below,
Love me sounded like a jest,
   Fit for *yes* or fit for *no*.

Call me false or call me free, —
   Vow, whatever light may shine,
No man on thy face shall see
   Any grief for change on mine.

Yet the sin is on us both :
   Time to dance is not to woo ;
Wooer light makes fickle troth ;
   Scorn of me recoils on you.

THE LADY'S YES.

Learn to win a lady's faith
   Nobly, as the thing is high ;
Bravely, as for life and death, —
   With a loyal gravity.

Lead her from the festive boards,
   Point her to the starry skies,
Guard her by your faithful words,
   Pure from courtship's flatteries.

By your truth she shall be true,
   Ever true, as wives of yore ;
And her Yes, once said to you,
   Shall be Yes forevermore.

A Health.

FILL this cup to one made up
  Of loveliness alone, —
A woman, of her gentle sex
  The seeming paragon;
To whom the better elements
  And kindly stars have given
A form so fair, that, like the air,
  'T is less of earth than heaven.

Her every tone is music's own,
  Like those of morning birds,
And something more than melody
  Dwells ever in her words;
The coinage of her heart are they,
  And from her lips each flows
As one may see the burdened bee
  Forth issue from the rose.

Affections are as thoughts to her,
  The measures of her hours;
Her feelings have the fragrancy,
  The freshness of young flowers;

And lovely passions, changing oft,
  So fill her, she appears
The image of themselves by turns, —
  The idol of past years!

Of her bright face one glance will trace
  A picture on the brain,
And of her voice in echoing hearts
  A sound must long remain;
But memory, such as mine of her,
  So very much endears,
When death is nigh, my latest sigh
  Will not be life's, but hers.

I fill this cup to one made up
  Of loveliness alone, —
A woman, of her gentle sex
  The seeming paragon;
Her health! and would on earth there stood
  Some more of such a frame,
That life might be all poetry,
  And weariness a name.

Winifred's Hair.

WINIFRED, waking in the morning,
  Locks dishevelled, sighed, "Alas!
Broken is the Venice-bodkin
  That you gave me — 't was of glass.
All my auburn hair, henceforward,
  Shall be given to the wind."
Ere the evening came, another's
  Net of pearl her hair confined.

Frail as the Venetian bauble
  I had thrust in Winifred's hair;
Lo! the net now snapped asunder,
  Other hands had fastened there.
Ere the moon's wide-blossomed petals
  On the breast of night had died,
Net and bodkin both deserted,
  Winifred's glittering hair flowed wide!

WINIFRED'S HAIR.

Silver comb and silken fillet
   Next in turn the wild hair bound.
Till at length the crown of wifehood
   Clasped its bands that hair around,—
Golden crown of Love! displacing
   Girlhood's vain adornments there.
Winifred never more shall alter,
   Now, the fashion of her hair.

In the Organ Loft.

THE dead in their ancient graves are still;
   There they've slept for many a year;
The last faint sunbeams glance o'er the hill,
   Gilding the dry grass, tall and sere,
And the foam of the babbling rill.

Into the church the ruddy light falls,
   Through rich stained windows, narrow and high;
Pictures it paints on the old gray walls,
   Scenes from the days that have long gone by, —
And hark! 't is my Rosalie calls!

She calls my name, — I have heard it oft
   Just at the golden sun's decline;
I answer the call, so sweet and soft;
   And, turning, see where her bright eyes shine,
High up in the organ loft.

I pass the winding and narrow stair;
   The gallery door stands open wide;
I know no shadow of pain or care,
   While darling Rosalie stands by my side,
In the sunset light so fair.

IN THE ORGAN LOFT.

What grand old hymns and chants we sang,
    Grand old chants that I loved so well!
And the organ's tones, — how they pealed and rang,
    Piercing the heart, no tongue can tell
With what a delicious pang!

Oh, those hours! what holy light
    Hovers around when their memories rise!
Music, love, and the sunset bright,
    Tenderest glances from Rosalie's eyes,
And a long, sweet kiss, for good-night!

A Garden in her Face.

THERE is a garden in her face,
    Where roses and white lilies grow;
A heavenly paradise is that place,
    Wherein all pleasant fruits do grow;
There cherries grow that none may buy,
Till cherry-ripe themselves do cry.

Those cherries fairly do inclose
    Of orient pearl a double row,
Which, when her lively laughter shows,
    They look like rose-buds filled with snow;
Yet these no peer nor prince may buy,
Till cherry-ripe themselves do cry.

Her eyes like angels' watch there still,
    Her brows like bended bows do stand,

Threatening with piercing frowns to kill
All that approach with eye or hand,
Those sacred cherries to come nigh,
Till cherry-ripe themselves do cry.

When Stars are in the Quiet Skies.

WHEN stars are in the quiet skies,
   Then most I pine for thee.
Bend on me then thy tender eyes,
   As stars look on the sea!
For thoughts, like waves that glide by night,
   Are stillest when they shine;
Mine earthly love lies hushed in light
   Beneath the heaven of thine.

There is an hour when angels keep
   Familiar watch o'er men,
When coarser souls are wrapped in sleep,—
   Sweet spirit, meet me then!
There is an hour when holy dreams
   Through slumber fairest glide;
And in that mystic hour, it seems
   Thou shouldst be by my side.

My thoughts of thee too sacred are
    For daylight's common beam:
I can but know thee as my star,
    My angel, and my dream!
When stars are in the quiet skies,
    Then most I pine for thee.
Bend on me then thy tender eyes,
    As stars look on the sea!

The Time I've Lost in Wooing.

The time I 've lost in wooing
    In watching and pursuing
        The light that lies
        In Woman's eyes,
Has been my heart's undoing.
Though Wisdom oft has sought me,
I scorned the lore she brought me;
        My only books
        Were Woman's looks,
And folly 's all they taught me.

Her smiles when Beauty granted,
I hung with gaze enchanted,
        Like him, the sprite,
        Whom maids by night
Oft meet in glen that 's haunted.
Like him, too, Beauty won me
But while her eyes were on me;
        If once their ray
        Was turned away,
Oh, winds could not outrun me!

THE TIME I'VE LOST IN WOOING.

And are those follies going?
And is my proud heart growing
   Too cold or wise
   For brilliant eyes
Again to set it glowing?
No,—vain, alas! th' endeavor
From bonds so sweet to sever;
   Poor Wisdom's chance
   Against a glance
Is now as weak as ever.

Not a Match.

KITTY, sweet and seventeen,
  Pulls my hair and calls me "Harry";
Hints that I am young and green,
  Wonders if I wish to marry.
Only tell me what reply
  Is the best reply for Kitty?
She 's but seventeen, and *I* —
  I am forty, — more 's the pity!

Twice at least my Kitty's age
  (Just a trifle over, maybe),
I am sober, I am sage,
  Kitty nothing but a baby.
She is merriment and mirth,
  I am wise and gravely witty;
She 's the dearest thing on earth,
  I am forty, — more 's the pity!

She adores my pretty rhymes,
  Calls me "poet" when I write them;

And she listens oftentimes
   Half an hour when I recite them.
Let me scribble by the page
   Sonnet, ode, or lover's ditty ;
Seventeen is Kitty's age,
   I am forty, — more 's the pity !

O SAW YE THE LASS?

SAW ye the lass wi' the bonny blue een?
   Her smile is the sweetest that ever was seen;
   Her cheek like the rose is, but fresher, I ween,
      She 's the loveliest lassie that trips on the green.
The home of my love is below in the valley,
Where wild-flowers welcome the wandering bee;
But the sweetest of flowers in that spot that is seen
Is the maid that I love wi' the bonny blue een.

When night overshadows her cot in the glen,
She 'll steal out to meet her loved Donald again;
And when the moon shines on the valley so green,
I 'll welcome the lass wi' the bonny blue een.
As the dove that has wandered away from his nest
Returns to the mate his fond heart loves the best,
I 'll fly from the world's false and vanishing scene,
To my dear one, the lass wi' the bonny blue een.

www.ingramcontent.com/pod-product-compliance
Lightning Source LLC
Chambersburg PA
CBHW030341170426
43202CB00010B/1204